Original title:
Frosted Reflections

Copyright © 2024 Swan Charm
All rights reserved.

Author: Eliora Lumiste
ISBN HARDBACK: 978-9916-79-471-5
ISBN PAPERBACK: 978-9916-79-472-2
ISBN EBOOK: 978-9916-79-473-9

A Tapestry of Frozen Thoughts

In the stillness, whispers float,
Threads of frost on a silver coat.
Captured dreams in a crystal haze,
Shimmer softly, in winter's gaze.

Each frozen moment, a story bound,
Nature weaves with a silence profound.
Fractals dance in the pale moonlight,
Weaving shadows that fade from sight.

Icy Traces of Lost Memories

Footsteps linger in the chilled air,
Echoes of laughter, now rare and fair.
Snowflakes drift on a fragile breeze,
Painting tales in the branches of trees.

Frosted windows, a view to the past,
Moments captured, yet slipping fast.
Memories held in the cold embrace,
Time distorts in this wintry space.

The Beauty in Crystal Stillness

A lake reflects the serene expanse,
Each ripple quiet, like a soft glance.
Glistening shards of the cool dawn,
Nature's canvas, delicately drawn.

The air so crisp, as the world holds breath,
In the calm, we dance with death.
Beauty blooms where the ice does lay,
In stillness, life finds its own way.

Enchanted Frost upon Still Waters

Silvery tendrils embrace the shore,
Whispers of magic, forevermore.
Frosty lace on the mirror's face,
Nature's secrets in quiet grace.

Reflections shimmer beneath the sheen,
A tranquil realm, pure and serene.
Beneath the stars, time stands still,
In enchanted dreams, our hearts fulfill.

Eclipsed by Frost's Gentle Touch

In silence, the night descends,
A blanket of frost, the world extends.
Stars shimmer softly, a silver embrace,
Nature holds breath, in this tranquil space.

Whispers of winter, the trees adorned,
Crystal crowns glisten, where dreams are born.
Footprints are delicate, the path is pure,
Frost's gentle touch, a beauty obscure.

Moonlight spills secrets on fields aglow,
Each glimmering shard, a tale to bestow.
Time seems to pause in the softest of nights,
Under the spell of ethereal lights.

A symphony delicate plays in the air,
As shadows and whispers dance without care.
Frozen reflections, a world out of reach,
Nature's soft canvas, she's ready to teach.

Awakening slowly, the dawn will descend,
The warmth of the sun begins to amend.
Yet memories linger, like frost on the glass,
A moment of wonder, forever to last.

Mirror'd Dreams on Glassy Lakes

In the heart of the morn, the water lies still,
Reflecting the skies with a magical thrill.
Crisp autumn leaves float, like whispers of gold,
Stories of seasons, in silence, retold.

Waves lap gently, a soft lullaby,
Echoes of dreams in the light-hued sky.
Mirrored horizons, where visions take flight,
Dance of the dawn, softening the night.

Ripples of wonder stretch out from the shore,
Each one a promise, a hope to explore.
Colors blend softly, in nature's embrace,
The lake holds a canvas, a fragile grace.

Fleeting reflections of days yet to come,
Life in the stillness, a heart softly drums.
Within the calm waters, the soul finds its way,
A journey of whispers at break of each day.

As sunlight awakens, it dances on glass,
Filling the world with a glow that will last.
In mirror'd dreams where the heart finds its home,
Nature's own secret, forever to roam.

Silent Shimmers

In the dark, a quiet gleam,
Whispers of a distant dream.
Stars above begin to sing,
Softly, light on fragile wing.

Moonlight dances on the lake,
Gentle ripples, hearts awake.
Silver threads of night unfold,
Stories of the brave and bold.

Flickering shadows, secrets hide,
In the stillness, dreams abide.
Every breath, a silent prayer,
In the night, we find our share.

Nature listens, peace descends,
In this space, the soul amends.
Silent shimmers, soft and bright,
Guiding us through endless night.

Winter's Gentle Veil

Snowflakes drift like whispered sighs,
Covering the earth, a soft disguise.
Barren branches, kissed by white,
In the stillness, pure delight.

Footsteps crunch on frozen ground,
In this silence, warmth is found.
Crisp air fills the lungs with cheer,
Nature's breath, both calm and clear.

Icicles hang like crystal dreams,
Reflecting sunlight's gentle beams.
Winter's touch, a timeless grace,
Drawing smiles on every face.

Fires crackle, stories shared,
By the hearth, hearts are bared.
In the glow, our spirits rise,
Winter's veil, a sweet surprise.

Crystal Echoes

Within the cave, a world of light,
Crystal echoes, pure and bright.
Nature's art, in colors spun,
Mirrored worlds, a dance begun.

Water drips, a melody,
Softly singing, wild and free.
Rays of sun through fractures play,
Illuminating magic's way.

Echoes whisper of the past,
Time's embrace, both deep and vast.
Each reflection tells a tale,
In this realm, we shall not fail.

Steps through shadows, light guides near,
Truth and wonder, banish fear.
Crystal echoes, nature's song,
In their arms, we all belong.

Glacial Glimmers

Icebergs drift in tranquil seas,
Whispers ride upon the breeze.
Sunlight kisses frozen skin,
Glimmers spark where dreams begin.

Shadows dance on sapphire waves,
Nature's beauty, wild and brave.
In the stillness, peace unfolds,
Stories waiting to be told.

Reflections of centuries past,
Moments held, forever cast.
Glimmers twinkle, bold and bright,
Anchoring hearts in flight.

Every tide, a heartbeat's pulse,
Rushing in, yet still, and dulcet.
Glacial glimmers, truth reveals,
In their grace, the world heals.

Sculpted in Ice

In winter's grasp, the world stands still,
Chiseled shapes on the icy hill.
Glassy figures, crisp and bright,
Shimmer softly in the light.

Snowflakes dance, a frozen lace,
Nature's art finds its place.
Silent whispers in the air,
Beauty crafted with such care.

Frigid touch of winter's breath,
Every curve brings life from death.
Moments caught, forever freeze,
Time is trapped in the deep freeze.

Fragments of the Past

Among the ruins, echoes play,
Whispering tales of yesterday.
Each stone tells a story lost,
Fragments found, but at what cost?

Dusty pages filled with light,
Glances back at endless night.
Memories like leaves in fall,
Each one answers passionate call.

Time has shaped these fragile threads,
Where dreams linger, and hope spreads.
Ghosts of laughter, tears that flow,
In every corner, histories glow.

The Essence of Cold

Chill drapes the night like a deep sigh,
Frosty whispers greet the shy.
Moonlight bathes the sleeping ground,
In its glow, peace can be found.

The heart of winter beats so slow,
In the stillness, secrets flow.
Breath of nature, crisp and clear,
Each moment layered, held so dear.

Silence wrapped in icy breath,
A quiet pause, a dance with death.
Within the cold, warmth seeks to rise,
As life awaits through frosty skies.

Seasons in Glass

Through a window, seasons change,
Each reflection feels so strange.
Spring blooms vibrant, life anew,
In each pane, a story true.

Summer's warmth, a golden hue,
Captured light in every view.
Autumn's leaves, a fiery dance,
Colors twirl, they take their chance.

Winter's chill, a silent grace,
Frosted patterns lace the space.
Each season framed 'neath the sky,
Moments held as days pass by.

Celestial Frost

Underneath the starry skies,
The frost begins to gently rise.
Crystals dance on branches bare,
A silent night, a breath of air.

Whispers echo through the trees,
Carried softly by the breeze.
Moonlight glimmers on the ground,
In this realm, magic is found.

Each flake glints, a diamond bright,
Painting shadows with its light.
The world wraps in silver lace,
A tranquil, fierce, and wondrous place.

In the stillness, time stands still,
Nature's beauty, pure and real.
With every breath, the magic grows,
In Celestial Frost, wonder flows.

As dawn approaches with its light,
The frost retreats, fading from sight.
Yet in our hearts, it will remain,
A memory of the winter's reign.

A Tapestry of Winter

Blankets white cover the ground,
A hush envelops all around.
Trees adorned with icy crowns,
Whispers of a world renowned.

Each flake falls from skies above,
Nature's gift, a gentle love.
Patterns weave on windows bright,
A tapestry of pure delight.

Footprints trail on frosty paths,
Echoes of the winter's laughs.
Children play, their joy unbound,
In this season's magic found.

As daylight fades to twilight's glow,
Stars awaken, putting on a show.
The night embraces, calm and clear,
In winter's arms, we draw near.

Through the cold, our hearts do warm,
In quiet moments, find the charm.
A tapestry that time can't sever,
Winter's song, a joy forever.

Refracted Whispers

Sunlight breaks through misty veils,
Creating patterns, light prevails.
Whispers of the day reborn,
In every drop, a new adorn.

Colors shimmer, dance, and sway,
In the quiet of the day.
Nature's voice, both soft and clear,
In refracted beams, we hear.

Each hue paints the world anew,
Fragments of a vibrant view.
Rainbows arch through summer skies,
Magic sparkles in our eyes.

With every whisper, tales unfold,
Mysteries of life retold.
In the shimmer, dreams take flight,
Refracted whispers, pure delight.

Beneath the glow, our spirits rise,
In the wonder, we realize.
Nature's canvas, bold and bright,
In refracted whispers, we find light.

Silvered Landscapes

Dawn unveils a silver scene,
Nature glistens, fresh and clean.
Mountains wear a gleaming crown,
Reflecting magic all around.

Each meadow sparkles in the sun,
Every journey has begun.
Footsteps tracing paths so clear,
In silvered landscapes, dreams appear.

Rivers shimmer, flowing bright,
Mirroring the sky's soft light.
The world transformed, serene and grand,
In nature's grasp, we understand.

With every breeze, the leaves do play,
In this landscape, we long to stay.
A canvas painted, bold and vast,
Moments cherished, shadows cast.

As daylight fades to starry nights,
The silver sparkles bring delights.
In silvered landscapes, we explore,
Nature's wonders, forevermore.

Artistry in Icy Splendor

Crystals dance in morning light,
Fractured shards of pure delight.
Nature's brush, a silent stroke,
Whispers of the cold, bespoke.

Glistening lakes, a mirror bright,
Reflecting dreams in purest white.
Each flake tells a tale anew,
Of winter's art, both calm and true.

Frozen branches, sculpted grace,
Nature's hands in lace embrace.
Softly falls the quiet snow,
Wrapped in beauty, time moves slow.

Sparkling nights with stars aligned,
In the chill, our hearts unwind.
The world transformed, so vast, so grand,
All in awe of nature's hand.

A fleeting glimpse of winter's glee,
In icy splendor, wild and free.
Moments carved in frosty air,
Masterpieces beyond compare.

Wisps of Light on a Chilled Surface

Moonlight dances on the lake,
Gentle ripples stir and wake.
Wisps of silver, soft and bright,
Glimmers on a chilled, clear night.

Branches whisper in the breeze,
Secrets shared among the trees.
Nature's peace, a calming grace,
Night's embrace, a warm embrace.

Each star a spark, a quiet song,
Guiding souls where they belong.
Reflections tell of dreams once dreamed,
In this beauty, we're redeemed.

A symphony of shadows play,
As dawn approaches, night gives way.
Golden hues begin to spread,
Painting paths where spirits tread.

In this moment, still and clear,
Wisps of light bring comfort near.
Chilled surface holds the night's embrace,
A tranquil heart finds its place.

The Poetry of Ice on Still Waters

Beneath the surface, silence dwells,
In mirrored depths, a tale it tells.
The poetry of ice profound,
In tranquil waters, peace is found.

Frozen whispers, stories old,
Captured dreams in crystal hold.
Nature's verses softly glow,
Eternal lines in frigid flow.

By the banks, the willows sway,
Framing views where swans ballet.
Each breath of wind brings grace anew,
In harmony, the world rings true.

Lost in thought, the heart takes flight,
Among the stillness, pure delight.
The dance of ice, the song of streams,
In nature's realm, we chase our dreams.

With every thaw, the tales release,
Life's pulse returns to seek its peace.
In poetry, this dance ignites,
In still waters, our spirits rise.

A Canvas of White Beneath the Stars

Blanketed fields in softest white,
Underneath the canvas of night.
Stars glitter like diamonds rare,
Painting visions in the air.

Snowflakes twirl in playful spree,
Each a gem, wild and free.
Every drift, a secret kept,
In winter's arms, memories slept.

A hush upon the world below,
In frozen beauty, hearts can grow.
Silhouettes of pines stand tall,
Guardians of an ancient call.

With every step, a crunch, a sound,
In this quiet, we are bound.
Beneath the stars, a story starts,
In nature's art, we find our hearts.

A canvas pure, a sight divine,
Where dreams and starlight intertwine.
In the stillness, hope takes flight,
A promise held in endless night.

The Art of Reflection

In the quiet of dusk,
Shadows dance and play,
Mirrors of the heart,
Whisper truths today.

Thoughts like flowing water,
Glistening in the light,
Each ripple holds a story,
Fading into night.

Gazing past the moment,
Time begins to blend,
Every glance a canvas,
Messages to send.

Within each soft silence,
Echoes of the past,
Painting all the memories,
A spell that holds fast.

In the art of stillness,
We find who we are,
Reflections guide our journey,
Like a shining star.

Timelessly Frozen

In the heart of winter,
Time stands still, awake,
Frosted breath of silence,
Nature's soft heartache.

Snowflakes gently falling,
Soft whispers on the ground,
A blanket of pure stillness,
Where peace can be found.

Icicles like sentinels,
Guarding secrets deep,
Frozen are the moments,
In a slumbering sleep.

Memories encased here,
In the chill we roam,
Wondering forever,
If this place is home.

Timelessly it lingers,
In each captured scene,
A world held in suspension,
Like a dream unseen.

In the Grip of Winter

Beneath the heavy clouds,
A blanket pure and white,
Nature's strong embrace holds,
All creatures wrapped tight.

The chilling wind whistles,
A song of icy breath,
Whispers of the season,
Mocking warmth of death.

Trees stand, stark and silent,
Their branches bare and cold,
Yet beauty finds its way,
In the stories told.

Fireplaces crackle bright,
Drawing hearts together,
In the grip of winter,
We find warmth in tether.

Moments shared in laughter,
While snowflakes swirl and spin,
In the heart of winter,
Life begins again.

Chill Veil of Memory

Glimmers of the past,
Wrapped in muted tones,
A chill veil of memory,
Whispers in soft tones.

Faded photographs speak,
Of laughter and of tears,
Each captures fleeting time,
Holding all our years.

Familiar voices linger,
Echoes through the hall,
Reminders of our journey,
We stumble and fall.

Time can be a thief,
Yet treasures remain clear,
Inside this chill veil,
Our loved ones draw near.

The heart's ache and beauty,
Intertwined so tight,
In the chill of memory,
We find warmth in light.

Ethereal Portraits

In skies of blue, the whispers play,
With colors bright, they dance and sway.
Each brushstroke tells a silent tale,
Of dreams unfurled in a cosmic veil.

The moonlight drapes on canvas bold,
While secrets of the night unfold.
Each shadow holds a fleeting glance,
A moment caught in a wistful trance.

The stars, they twinkle, soft and sweet,
In galleries where dreams do meet.
Their gentle glow, a guiding spark,
Illuminates the world in dark.

As time flows on, the portraits change,
Yet echoes of the past remain strange.
In every hue, a story lives,
In every line, the heart still gives.

With every sigh, a fresh start gleams,
In ethereal light, we weave our dreams.
A tapestry, both vast and small,
In the gallery of life, we stand tall.

Echoes of a Frozen Heart

In winter's breath, the silence grows,
A frozen realm, where no one knows.
The heartbeat slows, the pulse retreats,
In icy grips, the longing beats.

Each flake that falls, a tale untold,
Of love once warm, now bitter cold.
In shadows deep, the memories wake,
A haunting song the frost will make.

The echoes ring in twilight's glow,
Through crystal fields where whispers flow.
A heart once bold, now wrapped in frost,
In longing's dance, it counts the cost.

Each shimmer bright, a fleeting chance,
In winter's gloom, we seek romance.
Yet in the chill, the embers spark,
A flicker in the deepening dark.

With every breath, the frost might thaw,
Revealing hope, a silent law.
In echoes lost, we find a part,
The heartbeat stirs of a frozen heart.

Glinting at Dawn

As morning breaks, the light ignites,
A golden hue on distant heights.
The dewdrops twinkle, soft and bright,
In nature's dance, the day's delight.

The world awakens, sweet and slow,
With gentle winds that whisper low.
Each blade of grass, a vibrant song,
Entwines the heart where dreams belong.

The horizon blushes, colors blend,
In crimson rays, we find a friend.
The sun ascends, a fiery crown,
Bestowing warmth as shadows drown.

In glimmers soft, the hopes arise,
As light cascades through the painted skies.
With every breath, the promise keeps,
Awake in joy where silence weeps.

As day unfolds, the magic calls,
In every glow, a spirit sprawls.
In glinting morn, the souls will dance,
In radiant ways, we take our chance.

Veiled in Icy Grace

A shroud of frost upon the ground,
In crystals pure, a beauty found.
The world adorned in silver lace,
A frozen dream, in icy grace.

Each breath of wind, a tender sigh,
That weaves through branches, low and high.
In shimmering hues, the stillness sings,
As nature rests, the calmness clings.

With every step, the echoes call,
Of seasons past, where shadows fall.
Yet in this chill, a warmth remains,
In secret whispers, love sustains.

The delicate art of winter's hand,
Creates a realm, both vast and grand.
In beauty forged through harshest nights,
A dance of stars, the soul ignites.

As time slips by, the veil will fade,
Revealing warmth beneath the shade.
Yet in our hearts, the grace will stay,
A memory etched in ice and sway.

Nature's Quiet Canvas

In hues of green and gold,
The leaves dance in the breeze,
Upon the canvas wide,
Nature's art flows with ease.

Mountains rise like giants,
Their peaks touch the sky,
Whispers of the forest,
Beneath the clouds, they lie.

Rivers carve their pathways,
In patterns pure and clear,
Nature's brush keeps painting,
For all the world to cheer.

The sun dips low, a painter,
With colors bold and bright,
A masterpiece of twilight,
That ushers in the night.

And in this quiet moment,
Where time itself stands still,
Nature's beauty captures,
The heart, the mind, the will.

A Frozen Serenade

Snowflakes swirl like whispers,
In the still of the night,
Each flake a soft promise,
A dancer in the light.

Trees wear coats of shimmer,
As stars twinkle above,
A world wrapped in silence,
Embraced by winter's love.

The moon casts gentle shadows,
On the blanket of white,
While echoes of the evening,
Play notes of pure delight.

Frosty air, a canvas,
For breath to mist and fade,
A frozen serenade,
In the night softly made.

And as the dawn approaches,
With its golden ray,
The serenade of frost,
Illuminates the day.

Specters of Winter Light

Morning breaks, a shimmer,
On fields draped all in frost,
Specters dance in sunlight,
In beauty, we are lost.

Shadows of the pines stretch,
As the sun climbs higher,
A tapestry of warmth flows,
O'er land that looked so dire.

Birds sing their gentle ballads,
From branches stark and bare,
Echoes in the crisp air,
Woven with tender care.

Each flake, a ghostly whisper,
In the glow of winter's grace,
Painting tales of light and dark,
In this enchanted space.

As twilight draws the curtains,
On this fleeting sight,
We hold the memories close,
Of specular winter light.

The Art of Silence

In the hush of early dawn,
The world begins to wake,
A gentle breath of morning,
In stillness, hearts partake.

The rustle of the leaves,
A whisper in the breeze,
Nature speaks in silence,
A language meant to please.

Beneath the soaring heavens,
Where clouds drift soft and slow,
The art of silence dances,
In shadows cast below.

Moments weave like fabric,
A tapestry of thought,
In quiet contemplation,
Life's beauty is sought.

Listen close to silence,
Let its wisdom unfold,
For in its gentle grasp,
Lies a story yet untold.

Whispered Reflections

In the quiet hours of night,
Shadows dance with subtle light.
Softly echoes memories' song,
In the stillness, we belong.

Gentle winds weave through the trees,
Bringing whispers with the breeze.
Moments captured, time stands still,
Heartbeats fade, but dreams fulfill.

Moonlight bathes the earth in glow,
Painting stories soft and slow.
Each reflection tells a tale,
Of magic where the heart beats pale.

As the dawn begins to rise,
With the sun, new hopes arise.
Carried on the morning air,
Whispered thoughts beyond compare.

Finding peace in nature's grace,
In these quiet moments, space.
In the mirror of the night,
Whispers softly guide our flight.

Radiant Winter Gaze

See the world in winter's cloak,
Frosty breath where silence spoke.
Crystal flakes that shimmer bright,
Beneath the soft and silver light.

Mountains dressed in powdered white,
Glistening under stars so bright.
Footprints trace a tale untold,
In the chill, a warmth to hold.

Trees adorned with icy lace,
Nature's art, a tranquil space.
In the hush, a soft embrace,
Radiant wonders we can trace.

Breath of winter, crisp and clear,
In its beauty, we draw near.
Moments freeze as time extends,
In the cold, friendship transcends.

As the sun begins to rise,
Melting ice, a sweet surprise.
Winter's gaze starts to abate,
Radiant warmth we celebrate.

Subtle Hues Beneath Ice

Beneath the ice, the colors wait,
Woven dreams that time creates.
Subtle hues that softly blend,
Nature's palette, no end.

In the depths of winter's hold,
Mysteries in silence told.
Every shimmer, every shade,
Whispers secrets nature made.

Frozen lakes that mirror skies,
Catching glimpses, fleeting sighs.
Rippling waters, hidden grace,
Subtle beauty in this space.

As the thaw begins to break,
Life beneath the surface wakes.
Colors burst in soft reprise,
Beauty found in winter's guise.

Nature's hand with gentle touch,
Paints a world we love so much.
Beneath the ice, stories lie,
In the warmth, they start to fly.

The Beauty of Stillness

In the stillness, find your peace,
Time stands still; the world will cease.
Breath of nature, soft and slow,
In the quiet, love shall grow.

Softly falling leaves at dusk,
Whispers of the night's sweet musk.
Each heartbeat resonates within,
Where the silence does begin.

Stars above twinkle with grace,
In the dark, a warm embrace.
Moments linger, sweet and bright,
In the beauty of the night.

Still waters reflect the moon,
Gentle echo, nature's tune.
Savoring what life bestows,
In the calm, our spirit flows.

Embrace the stillness, let it stay,
In the hush, we find our way.
Beauty lies in moments wispy,
In the quiet, life feels crispy.

Quicksilver Dreams

In whispers of the night,
The stars begin to gleam,
Chasing shadows in flight,
We weave our quicksilver dream.

A dance upon the edge,
Where light and darkness play,
We walk a fragile ledge,
In dusk's enchanting sway.

With every breath we share,
The world begins to fade,
A memory of air,
In twilight's gentle parade.

Through valleys of our hopes,
We navigate the streams,
On silver-laden slopes,
We craft our quicksilver dreams.

Awake in the dawn's light,
The magic slips away,
Yet still, in fleeting sight,
Our dreams will boldly stay.

Reflected in the Cold

Beneath a glassy lake,
The world is held so still,
Each breath a gentle ache,
A frozen, dream-like thrill.

In winter's soft embrace,
The secrets lie concealed,
With every frosty trace,
A memory revealed.

We wander through the fog,
In silence, hearts unfold,
Each moment, like a log,
Reflected in the cold.

The echoes of the past,
Dance lightly on the ice,
A beauty unsurpassed,
In this serene paradise.

The chill begins to fade,
As warmth creeps in the day,
Yet still, the dreams we've made,
In frost will softly stay.

Soft Glimmers of Time

In gentle morning light,
Time whispers in our ears,
Unfurling day from night,
We gather all our years.

Moments like grains of sand,
Slip softly through our hands,
We trace the lines so grand,
In life's shifting strands.

Soft glimmers in the dusk,
Memories left behind,
Each heartbeat, a fine musk,
In the labyrinth of mind.

We chase the fleeting hours,
As shadows start to blend,
With love's ephemeral flowers,
Time will be our friend.

In twilight's soft embrace,
We hold what's fleeting tight,
For in this sacred space,
We dance in soft twilight.

The Silence of Ice

In the hush of the dawn,
The world breathes pure and slow,
Where labels are all gone,
And only silence flows.

The ice wraps every sound,
In cold and tranquil grace,
We find our thoughts unbound,
In this ethereal space.

A glimmer starts to form,
On frozen rivers' edge,
The stillness, like a norm,
A sacred, silent pledge.

In winter's soft embrace,
We wander far and wide,
Through beauty's sacred space,
With silence as our guide.

The echoes fade away,
In icy realms we roam,
For in this calm display,
We find a fleeting home.

Glacial Dreams

In the stillness of the night,
Where shadows float in pale light,
Whispers of ice drift and sway,
Glacial dreams come out to play.

Frozen lakes beneath the moon,
Mirrored skies in silver tune,
Endless silence clings like breath,
Chill of winter, dance with death.

Mountains echo, stark and clear,
Calling forth the summer's cheer,
Yet the frost holds tight its reign,
In this land of crystal pain.

A tapestry of white and blue,
Crafted by the cold's soft hue,
Nature's canvas, bold and grand,
Frozen art in quiet land.

Windswept valleys weave with grace,
Ghostly shapes in endless space,
Here in dreams, the heart's set free,
Glacial realms, my solemn plea.

Unearthed in Snow

Beneath the blanket, secrets rest,
Silent tales of winter's quest,
Footprints lost in soft white veil,
Unearthed dreams in snow prevail.

Crystal whispers, soft like sighs,
The world sleeps as the dark sky flies,
Nature holds its breath in peace,
In this calm, all worries cease.

Echoes of laughter, far and near,
Drift like snowflakes, light and clear,
Every flake tells tales untold,
As stories of the past unfold.

Branches heavy, bowed with weight,
Nature's gifts from heaven's gate,
In their arms, the world embraces,
The cold beauty that it traces.

From the earth, a quiet hum,
Calling forth the ages' drum,
In the stillness where life flows,
Unearthed dreams in quiet snows.

Echoing Across the Ice

Voices linger, lost in air,
Echoing across the fair,
Frozen whispers, soft and bright,
Carrying tales through the night.

Every crack beneath my feet,
Sings a song, a steady beat,
Nature's symphony unfolds,
In the cold, a truth retold.

Shadows dance on glistening white,
Merging spirits in the light,
Icebound realms, a world so vast,
Memories of the frozen past.

Mountain peaks reach for the stars,
Wonders held behind cold bars,
Echoes chase the fleeting day,
In the icy grip, they sway.

Time stands still where hopes abide,
On the glacier's frozen slide,
Echoing, our dreams take flight,
Across the vast, enchanting night.

Shimmering Moments

In the dawn, the world awakes,
Every breath, a chance it takes,
Sunrise paints the frosty ground,
Shimmering moments, magic found.

Every flake that drifts and glows,
Carries warmth in winter's throes,
Gentle light on snowflakes glint,
Nature's brush, a soft imprint.

Through the trees, the sunlight streams,
Crystal glories, woven dreams,
Laughter echoes in the air,
Shimmering moments everywhere.

Time slips by on winter's breeze,
Magic lingers in the freeze,
Hourglass sands of silver dust,
In these moments, we must trust.

Even as the shadows fall,
Hope is spoken, a quiet call,
Shimmering dreams, forever stay,
In our hearts, they light the way.

Silent Crystals on the Glass

Silently they glimmer bright,
Hiding secrets, soft in light.
Captured dreams in frozen lace,
Whispers of a cold embrace.

Facets sharp, yet delicate,
In their stillness, hearts await.
Nature's breath a breathless sigh,
Beneath the frosty, azure sky.

Every edge like time stands still,
As the world bends to their will.
Frozen echoes, sweetly spun,
Silent tales of day begun.

In the morning's golden glow,
Silent crystals come to show.
Quiet wonders, nature's art,
Cold reflections, warm the heart.

Whispering Thorns of Winter

Beneath the snow, the thorns do sleep,
Guarding dreams that silence keeps.
Whispers soft in shadows sway,
Breath of winter, cold and grey.

Crimson berries, bold, declare,
Promises of springtime's dare.
Thorns embrace the frostbit night,
Cradling hopes away from sight.

Twisted branches, stark and bare,
Weaving tales in chilling air.
Whispers share a future bright,
In the depths of winter's bite.

Against the dark, they stand, they fight,
Holding close the coming light.
Whispered stories gently flow,
Through the thorns where love can grow.

Shattered Mirrors of Ice

In the silence, shards are found,
Fractured dreams on frozen ground.
Reflecting light in scattered ways,
A dance of darkness, winter's maze.

Each piece tells a story lost,
Echoes of what love had crossed.
In the glimmer, pain shines bright,
Shattered mirrors, breaking light.

Beauty lingers in the cracks,
Hints of strength in fragile tracks.
Through the winter's bitter chill,
Hope emerges, steadied will.

Ice will melt, the truth will rise,
From the shards, new visions prize.
In the warmth of springtime's breath,
Life reborn from frozen death.

Glistening Veils of the Dawn

Veils of mist in morning's glow,
Whisper secrets soft and low.
Nature wakes with gentle grace,
In the light, we find our place.

Golden threads in sky unspool,
Painting dreams in radiant jewel.
Birds take flight on whispered wings,
Melodies of dawn, it sings.

Glistening dew on emerald leaves,
Sings the song that nature weaves.
Every drop a world refines,
In this moment, life aligns.

Through the haze of morning light,
Softly fades the cloak of night.
Glistening veils, a fresh new start,
Wrap the day in nature's art.

The Chill of Silent Echoes

In shadows deep, the whispers dwell,
The night becomes a tale to tell.
Soft fingers grazed the icy air,
Each breath a ghost that lingers there.

A hollow sound, a distant beat,
Where time and memory softly meet.
The chill wraps close, a gentle sigh,
As stars blink softly in the sky.

Fractured lights through branches weave,
A tapestry of night, believe.
The echo fades, yet lingers still,
In quiet thoughts that hearts fulfill.

The world sleeps on, in silent grace,
While echoes dance, they leave no trace.
A shiver runs through ancient trees,
In lands untouched by warming freeze.

So let the night resound with truth,
In echo's grip, there lies our youth.
For every chill, a warmth awaits,
In silent rhythms, fate creates.

Murmurs in a Glacial Breeze

A breeze that whispers secrets low,
On icy paths where soft winds blow.
Each note a tale, so lightly spun,
Beneath the veil of winter's sun.

Branches sway, as if to dance,
To melodies of frozen chance.
The murmurs twine like silver thread,
In shadows where the light has fled.

Frosted breaths from lips of dreams,
In glacial waves, the silence seems.
The world stands still, in twilight's hand,
As whispers weave through winter's land.

Crystals glitter, quiet and bright,
Murmuring softly through the night.
A harmony of cold and calm,
That wraps the earth in winter's psalm.

So listen close, to every breeze,
For in the chill, the heart finds ease.
In murmurs small, there shines the truth,
A song of calm that holds our youth.

Translucent Dreams of December

In twilight's glow, the dreams unfold,
Through layers soft, a tale retold.
The air is thick with hopes and sighs,
Where memories linger, softly rise.

Translucent skies, a canvas clear,
Each twinkling star, a whispered cheer.
As shadows blend with winter's grace,
In December's heart, we find our place.

A world transformed by frost's embrace,
Time slips away without a trace.
Caught in the web of silver lace,
We lose ourselves in this still space.

The dreams cascade like falling snow,
In gentle flurries, fast or slow.
Each flake a wish, each breath a spark,
Illuminating dreams from dark.

So let us dance in winter's light,
With translucent dreams as our delight.
In December's arms, we find our way,
Through fragile paths of night and day.

Woven Threads of Winter's Embrace

In twilight's grip, the stories weave,
Through snowy drifts, the spirits cleave.
A tapestry of frost and sighs,
Each moment captured, softly lies.

The chill encircles, close and beat,
In whispered tones, the echoes greet.
Woven threads of dreams entwined,
In winter's hold, our paths aligned.

The nights stretch long, with starlit glow,
Where shadows blend with crystal snow.
With every heartbeat, warmth ignites,
In woven tales of frosty nights.

A quiet dance beneath the trees,
With every breath, the spirit frees.
In winter's charm, together we chase,
The woven threads of time and space.

So hold this warmth, as shadows play,
In winter's arms, we'll find our way.
With every thread, a story spun,
In this embrace, we are as one.

Reflections in a Winter's Gaze

Cold winds brush against my face,
Gentle flakes begin to race.
Silent footsteps lead me near,
Mirrored dreams in white so clear.

Pine trees stand, a stoic guard,
Against the chill, they bear the hard.
Footprints trace a tale unspoken,
In this quiet, hearts are broken.

Sunrise breaks on icy streams,
Glints of hope in frozen dreams.
Nature's breath, a whispered song,
In winter's hold, we all belong.

Shadows dance as daylight fades,
In this world, true peace pervades.
Reflections deep, the heart will know,
In the stillness, love will glow.

Echoes of a Frozen Whisper

Through the trees, a frosty sigh,
Softly whispered, drifting by.
Echoes linger, long and clear,
Nature's call, so sweet to hear.

Crystals sparkle in the light,
Each a tale of winter's bite.
Secrets hidden in the chill,
A quiet strength, a steadfast will.

Mountains dressed in coats of white,
Dancing under soft moonlight.
Footsteps crunch on freshly laid,
In that moment, fears allayed.

Stars above, a guiding hand,
In the hush, we make our stand.
Echoes meld with heartbeats soft,
In frozen stillness, spirits loft.

Illuminated Paths in the Snow

A path unfolds in gentle glow,
Underneath the falling snow.
Footsteps light on frosty ground,
Whispers of the night abound.

Lanterns flicker, shadows sway,
As the night transforms the day.
Each step forward brings the light,
Turning darkness into bright.

Silent woods, a peaceful throng,
Every heartbeat, nature's song.
Golden glimmers, soft and warm,
Within this realm, we find our charm.

Beneath the stars, our dreams take flight,
In winter's blanket, pure delight.
Illuminated, hearts entwined,
On this journey, love defined.

Shards of Light Through Winter's Mist

Through the fog, shards of gold,
Winter's mystique, tales retold.
Glimmers pierce the icy veil,
Guiding souls who cannot fail.

Frosty breath in morning's air,
Promises of warmth, a rare affair.
Nature's canvas, white and bright,
In the distance, hope ignites.

Silent whispers through the trees,
Carried softly on the breeze.
Moments shared, a lover's touch,
In the quiet, we feel so much.

Echoes of a world awake,
In the stillness, hearts shall shake.
Shards of light through misty night,
Winter's bond, a pure delight.

Nature's Silent Cradle of Snow

Beneath a quilt of white, so pure,
Nature sleeps, its dreams secure.
Whispers of the wind may sigh,
In the cradle, time drifts by.

Trees bend low with heavy lace,
In winter's calm, they find their place.
Footprints mark the world outside,
Secrets in the snow abide.

The brook flows slow, its voice a hum,
In icy depths, the echoes come.
Frosted breath of morning light,
Cradles dreams till day is bright.

Softly falls the snow anew,
Blanketing the earth in hue.
Nature rests, a peaceful art,
In silence, whispers to the heart.

So let us cherish winter's gift,
In every snowfall, spirits lift.
For in the stillness, life shall grow,
In nature's silent cradle of snow.

Luminous Patterns on a Frigid Night

Stars ignite the velvet sky,
A silent dance, they spin and fly.
Moonlight spills on frozen ground,
In this beauty, peace is found.

Crystals form in chilly air,
Luminous patterns everywhere.
Branches wear an ice-cold crown,
Glistening in the night's deep gown.

With every breath, we see the glow,
A world transformed by frost and snow.
Whispers echo, soft and light,
In magic's hold on this frigid night.

Each step taken feels like grace,
In winter's arms, we find our place.
The night holds secrets, calm and bright,
In luminous patterns, pure delight.

So let us roam beneath the stars,
Embracing winter's beauty, ours.
For in the dark, we rise, take flight,
With luminous patterns on a frigid night.

The Essence of Stillness in Winter

Silence blankets every tree,
In winter's heart, we find the key.
Footfalls muffled, world at peace,
In stillness, all our worries cease.

Clouds cocoon the fleeting sun,
As daylight whispers, day is done.
Night unveils its starry cloak,
In the stillness, spirits woke.

Snowflakes dance, a gentle cheer,
Embracing all who wander near.
Nature's breath in sync with time,
The essence found in every rhyme.

From frozen lakes to icy streams,
Stillness weaves through all our dreams.
Winter holds a sacred space,
Where time slows down, and we find grace.

Let us linger in this calm,
In winter's grasp, we find our balm.
With every heartbeat, hope ignites,
The essence of stillness in winter nights.

Glimmers of Hope in a Snowstorm

The blizzard roars, the winds a howl,
Yet within, a softness, nature's prowl.
As snowflakes dance in wild delight,
Glimmers of hope emerge in white.

Every flake a story spun,
Filling voids where light is shunned.
In whirling storms, we seek a sign,
Amongst the chaos, hearts align.

Branches bow, yet do not break,
Resilience found for hope's own sake.
Through swirling winds and endless night,
Glimmers appear, a beacon bright.

So hold on tight as tempests roar,
Let love and hope become your core.
For in the heart of winter's storm,
Glimmers await, in every form.

In snowy depths, our spirits rise,
As whispers of the storm advise.
With every gust, a chance to soar,
Glimmers of hope forevermore.

Tales from an Icy Mirror

In the twilight's soft embrace,
Reflections dance on glassy face.
Whispers echo, secrets told,
In winter's grasp, the world turns cold.

Fractured dreams on frosted ground,
Stories lost, yet still abound.
Amidst the chill, old legends weave,
In every breath, hope to believe.

Crystals shimmer in pale moonlight,
Casting shadows, ghostly sight.
Through frozen paths, the echoes flow,
Carrying warmth from long ago.

Silent woods, a canvas bare,
Nature's art, beyond compare.
Each heartbeat sings a hidden tune,
Beneath the watchful, silver moon.

Lurking doubts in crisp night air,
Yet dreams ignite beyond despair.
In this mirror, stories gleam,
Life's frozen trace, a haunting dream.

Silhouettes of Nightfall in Frost

Velvet skies where shadows creep,
Softly snows the silence deep.
Frosted branches raise their arms,
In night's embrace, the cold still charms.

Moonlight spills on fields of white,
Casting peace in darkened night.
Footprints linger, tales unwind,
Whispers of the past confined.

Silhouettes in icy glow,
Ghostly figures weaving slow.
Nature hums a timeless tune,
Embraced by chill 'neath silver moon.

Stars peer down, a watchful crowd,
Secrets wrapped in winter's shroud.
As moments freeze, the heart beats strong,
In silence shared, we all belong.

Fingers trace the frozen panes,
Each line drawn holds quiet pains.
But in the chill, a warmth is sown,
In every heart, we're never alone.

A Serenade of Silver and White

Notes of frost, a gentle hum,
Through the trees, the winter strums.
Whispers soft, the night enfolds,
A serenade of silver holds.

Winter's breath, a chilling sigh,
Fingers trace the frosty sky.
Each flake dances, pure delight,
In the hush of soft twilight.

Branches bow with snowy lace,
Nature's tune, a sacred space.
Harmony flows, against the chill,
In the stillness, hearts are filled.

Footsteps echo, crisp and clear,
In this song, we have no fear.
Underneath the starry veil,
Winter whispers, love will prevail.

As silence falls, the world is bright,
With every breath, a spark ignites.
Together here, we stand, unite,
In this serenade, we take flight.

Captured Breath of Winter's Breath

A breath of frost upon the air,
Nature's art, a silent prayer.
In every exhale, cold and clear,
Winter whispers, drawing near.

Captured moments in soft glaze,
Reflecting life in winter's daze.
Frozen echoes stir the soul,
While time stands still, eternally whole.

Through valleys wrapped in quiet peace,
Each heartbeat finds a sweet release.
The world adorned in icy white,
Breath by breath, we feel the night.

Snowflakes swirl, a dance divine,
In shadows cast from trees that twine.
A fleeting glance, yet timeless span,
In every flake, the touch of man.

As branches sway in cold moonlight,
The whispers of the stars ignite.
In frosty breath, life finds a thread,
Weaving warmth where once was dread.

Crystalized Thoughts

In the silence of the mind,
Ideas take their flight,
Glistening like the stars,
In the calm of night.

Captured in a moment,
A whisper in the air,
Fleeting as the shadows,
Of dreams that linger there.

Thoughts emerge like crystals,
Fragile yet so bright,
Reflecting all the wonders,
Of a tranquil sight.

Caught in webs of longing,
Each glimmer tells a tale,
Of hopes that weave and wander,
On a gentle gale.

In the heart's deep chamber,
These treasures find their place,
A gallery of moment,
In time's soft embrace.

The Winter's Glow

Amidst the falling snow,
A warmth begins to rise,
Night wraps its arms around,
As the moon softly sighs.

Fires crackle gently,
Casting shadows that dance,
On walls adorned with memories,
Of winter's sweet romance.

Breath of frost hangs thick,
In the crisp, cold night air,
Yet hearts glow ever brighter,
With a love we gladly share.

Footsteps crunch on pathways,
Leading to dreams unheard,
Each moment a heartbeat,
In the silent world, stirred.

Wrapped in gentle whispers,
We find our steady pace,
Through the chilling beauty,
Of this winter's embrace.

Traces of White

Over fields, a quiet hush,
Blankets draped so fine,
Nature wears a crystal coat,
In the softest design.

Trees stand stark and silent,
Their limbs a frozen lace,
Each branch a work of art,
In winter's pure grace.

The world slows to a whisper,
Every sound refined,
Echoes of the past,
In the chill of the wind.

Footprints mark the journey,
Of wanderers like us,
Leaving traces where we've been,
In the snow's gentle hush.

As daylight starts to fade,
The horizon glows bright,
A soft reminder that,
We're never out of sight.

Time in Suspended Ice

Moments frozen, caught in glass,
Each tick a silent plea,
Time stands still in sacred space,
A slip of eternity.

Icicles like crystal fingers,
Point towards the sky,
Holding on to what once was,
As the days go by.

Layers grip the memories,
Shells of moments past,
In this thrum of quietude,
Where shadows often cast.

Suspended in this stillness,
Life waits with bated breath,
In the calm, a promise stirs,
Renewal after death.

So let us linger here awhile,
In beauty's frozen grace,
For time will soon release us,
To chase another space.

Gleaming Silhouettes

In the dusk where shadows play,
Silent whispers greet the day.
Figures dance in silver light,
Dreams take wing, ready for flight.

Trees stand tall like sentinels,
Guarding secrets, casting spells.
Stories linger in the air,
Carried softly, everywhere.

The moon spills gold upon the ground,
Glimmers scattered all around.
Nature wraps us in its shroud,
Moments cherished, proud and loud.

Echoes of a day gone by,
Reading into the starry sky.
Memories twine like vines on stone,
In the heart, we're never alone.

As night falls with its velvet grace,
We find solace in this space.
Each silhouette, a tale untold,
In this realm where dreams unfold.

Crystalized Memories

Frozen drops from time's embrace,
In each shard, a sacred place.
Glimmers of laughter, tears, and sighs,
Captured moments never die.

A blink of joy caught in the light,
A shadow cast with soft delight.
Laughter dances in the frost,
Every heartbeat, never lost.

Footfalls echo on the ground,
In these frames, our dreams are found.
Time stands still, a perfect blend,
Crystal tales that gently mend.

Remembered whispers in the air,
Fleeting glimpses, always rare.
Crafting worlds where we belong,
In this stillness, life's sweet song.

The past and present intertwine,
In every memento, love will shine.
Let these memories softly glow,
In the heart, forever flow.

Reflections in the Frost

Windows fogged with secret dreams,
Nature weaves her icy seams.
Frosted patterns on the glass,
Remind us of the moments past.

Silent mornings whisper clear,
Each reflection drawing near.
In the chill, we see our grace,
Fleeting smiles upon each face.

Time suspended, beautifully still,
Every breath a quiet thrill.
Captured in a shimmering frame,
Life's brief dance, a whispered name.

Through the ice, our stories flow,
Secrets only winter know.
Glistening sights, a whispered lore,
In each frost, we love once more.

As sunlight breaks the cold embrace,
Warmth returns to weary space.
Reflections fade with time's soft hand,
But in our hearts, forever stand.

The Chill's Portrait

Brush of frost on winter's breath,
A living canvas, life and death.
Crisp air carries tales untold,
In every chill, a heart of gold.

The trees, they wear a cloak of white,
Guarding dreams through the night.
Colors muted, yet so bright,
In this quiet, pure delight.

Ice crystals twinkle, spirits soar,
Every flake, a hidden lore.
Moments caught in winter's art,
Each a fragment of the heart.

Solitude in the biting chill,
Reflecting stillness, peace until.
The world sleeps under cold's embrace,
In this time, we find our place.

Through the frost, we shape our dreams,
A tapestry of silent seams.
Each chill a brushstroke on the skin,
The portrait painted deep within.

Gleaming Landscapes in a Silver Haze

Morning mist drapes the hills,
A silver sheen on quiet streams,
Whispers of light through the trees,
Nature's lullaby softly gleams.

Mountains wear a frosted crown,
Sunrise dances on the frost,
Shadows play as day comes round,
A fleeting beauty, never lost.

Fields stretch wide, a waltz of white,
Beneath the sky's vast, tender gaze,
Every flake a dream in flight,
In gleaming landscapes, we wander, amazed.

Footprints trace the frozen ground,
A chorus of memories unfolds,
Stories whispered all around,
In this realm where magic holds.

Underneath the silver beams,
Hope awakens from its rest,
In the hush, we find our dreams,
Gleaming landscapes, nature's best.

Faint Imprints on a Frozen Canvas

In the twilight's gentle fade,
Footprints linger, soft and pale,
Faint sketches on nature's page,
A story told through winter's veil.

Brush of snowflakes, soft and light,
Covering the world in grace,
Each hushed moment, pure delight,
On this canvas, time finds its place.

Branches wear their frosted lace,
Beneath the weight, they bow so low,
Faint imprints where dreams embrace,
A silent waltz through falling snow.

Night descends, the stars ignite,
Inky black, a twinkling sea,
Beneath their gaze, hearts take flight,
Faint imprints of what will be.

Whispers echo through the cold,
Promises in every sigh,
Stories of the brave, the bold,
On this canvas, we can fly.

Chasing Shadows of Frostbitten Dreams

In the stillness of the night,
Shadows dance in icy grace,
Chasing whispers, soft and light,
Frostbitten dreams we long to trace.

Moonlight glimmers on the snow,
Dreams emerge in silver hues,
Through the chill, we feel the glow,
Chasing shadows, fleeting views.

Every flake a hope reborn,
Every sigh a wish, a plea,
In the quiet, hearts are worn,
Frostbitten dreams, wild and free.

Footsteps echo on this path,
Leading through a realm unseen,
With each breath, a gentle laugh,
As we wander in between.

In the dark, we find our way,
Guided by the stars above,
Chasing shadows, come what may,
Frostbitten dreams fueled by love.

The Lure of Winter's Crystal Heart

Icebound branches glimmer bright,
Nature's jewels, a frosty crown,
Whispers call in the pale light,
The lure of winter, softly sounds.

Each corner holds a secret form,
Under blankets of snow so deep,
A tranquil hush, a heartfelt norm,
In this stillness, our souls steep.

Amidst the chill, a fire burns,
Passions rise in frosty air,
With every turn, the heart learns,
The beauty found in winter's glare.

Footprints in the glittering frost,
A path that leads to dreams anew,
Finding warmth where love is lost,
In winter's heart, we will break through.

Crystals shimmer, soft and pure,
Embracing all we hold so dear,
The lure of winter, sweet and sure,
In its heart, we cast off fear.

Icy Whispers

In the stillness of night, cold winds sigh,
Soft secrets float on frosty clouds high.
Moonlight dances on snow-kissed ground,
Nature's voice in whispers profound.

Each breath a crystal, fragile and bright,
Echoes of warmth fade into the night.
Footsteps muffled on glittering trails,
In winter's embrace, the heart never fails.

Stars twinkle above, like diamonds they gleam,
Icy whispers weave through a silvery dream.
Frozen shadows, a hushed lullaby,
Under the blanket where secrets lie.

Branches adorned with a delicate lace,
Nature's artistry, a serene embrace.
With every heartbeat, the world holds its breath,
In the realm of winter, we dance with death.

So let us wander where north winds play,
In icy whispers, we'll find our way.
Each flake a promise, a story untold,
In the chilling silence, our dreams unfold.

Mirror of the Chill

Reflections dance on a crystal lake,
Where frigid waters stir and shake.
The trees stand tall with frosted crowns,
Guardians of silence in winter's frowns.

Glimmers of ice in the morning light,
Nature's jewels, in purest sight.
Each branch a mirror, a story to tell,
Capturing moments where dreams softly dwell.

Shadows cast by the waning sun,
In the chill of twilight, the day is done.
Echoes of laughter, now far away,
In the mirror of chill where memories sway.

Footprints etched in the soft white snow,
Lead us to places only we know.
Under the frost, a heartbeat remains,
In the mirror's depths, love softly gains.

With every sigh of the winter's breath,
We weave through time, embracing the depth.
In the mirror of chill, our spirits fly free,
Reflected in moments, just you and me.

Shattered Glass Dreams

A cascade of colors, sharp and bright,
Fragments of dreams caught in the light.
Like crystal petals scattered around,
Whispers of hopes, in silence they sound.

In every shard, a story is spun,
Reflections of battles lost but won.
Each piece a memory, a laugh, a tear,
Shattered glass dreams, so precious, so dear.

Time intertwines with the fragile glass,
Moments we cherish, they fleetingly pass.
Through the chaos, a beauty appears,
In shattered reflections, we conquer our fears.

As sunlight breaks through in golden streams,
Fractured memories glow with new dreams.
In each twisted angle, a smile will rise,
Beauty born from the pain in our eyes.

So gather the pieces, let the light in,
From shattered glass dreams, we begin again.
Each fragment a canvas, unique in its way,
In the dance of the light, we find our own sway.

The Hushed Embrace

In the quiet of dusk, shadows entwine,
Wrapped in the warmth of love's soft design.
Whispers linger like stars in the night,
Promises shared in the pale moonlight.

Through the silence, our hearts take flight,
Bathed in the glow of calm delight.
With every heartbeat, we find our place,
Bound in the magic of a hushed embrace.

Time slows down in this sacred space,
Fingers entwined, no need to race.
In every glance, a world anew,
Two souls waltzing, forever true.

Wrapped in affection, the night unfolds,
Tales of our journeys quietly told.
In the stillness, we carve our dreams,
Life dances gently within its seams.

So let us linger where whispers reside,
In the beauty of love, let our hearts guide.
In the hushed embrace, we find our way,
Together in silence, forever we stay.

Resonance of Cold in a Warm Heart

In the hush of winter's breath,
Embers glow beneath the frost,
Whispers chirp in quiet nests,
Warmth found where love is lost.

Snowflakes dance like fleeting dreams,
Brushing softly on the skin,
Fires flicker, gently gleam,
Hope ignites where hearts begin.

Lingering scent of cedar wood,
Wrapped in blankets stitched with care,
Songs of solace, understood,
Resonance blooms in evening air.

Time suspends in gilded light,
Voices blend, a sweet refrain,
Holding close the starry night,
Defying all the world's disdain.

Melodies of warmth awake,
Together in the silent fall,
With every breath, we softly make,
A universe that calls us all.

Tales of Ice and Whispering Winds

Beneath the veil of shimmering white,
Icicles hang like frozen tears,
The wind through pines begins to write,
Tales of solitude and fears.

Mountains wrapped in icy shrouds,
Secrets drift with every gust,
Whispers draw from snowy clouds,
In nature's grasp, we place our trust.

Winds caress the stark terrain,
Echoes linger, faint and clear,
Memories etched in crystal rain,
In each flake, a story near.

Footprints lead to paths once walked,
Frostbite sharpens every sound,
In the silence, shadows talked,
To the heart, a tale unbound.

Together, across the frozen lakes,
We weave the night, we seize the day,
In every breeze, a bond awakes,
Chasing sunbeams on our way.

Fragments of Light in a Frozen World

In the quiet of morning light,
Crystals form on branches bare,
Every gleam, a fleeting sight,
Whispers of the frosty air.

Fractured rays through ice-cold glass,
Scattering warmth on wintry days,
Time reflected as moments pass,
In a world of white and grays.

Sunrise paints the hills anew,
Beneath a sky of crystal blue,
Hopes like shadows flicker through,
In the bleakness, brave hearts grew.

Frosted paths with secrets paved,
Breathe in deep the chilling air,
In this realm, where dreams are saved,
Every heartbeat spins a prayer.

In the stillness, life persists,
Fragments glisten, souls entwined,
In frozen moments, truth exists,
Warmth of spirit redefined.

Dance of the Icicles

Hanging low from rooftops high,
Icicles sway in frosty air,
Sparkling under azure sky,
A ballet, delicate and rare.

Each drip a note in winter's tune,
Resonating with the breeze,
Graceful as the fading moon,
Weaving whispers through the trees.

Crystalline chandeliers aglow,
Dancing softly, tumbling down,
In their flight, a gentle flow,
Cascading beauty all around.

Frost-kissed fingers hold the night,
Each glimmer sings of what's to be,
A fleeting waltz of shadowed light,
In the heart, they set us free.

From darkness blooms a tender spark,
As nature bows to winter's call,
In the silence, dreams embark,
To dance in night's embrace, we fall.

Elusive Solitude

In shadows deep, I seek the light,
Whispers soft, they take their flight.
A world apart, so vast and wide,
In silence deep, I choose to bide.

Alone I wander, paths unknown,
Among the trees, where dreams are sown.
The echoes call, a gentle plea,
In this stillness, I am free.

With every leaf, I find my way,
Through tangled thoughts that lead astray.
In nature's heart, I shed my guise,
In tranquil peace, my spirit rise.

Birdsong lingers in the air,
Softly wrapping me in care.
Each breath a dance, a sacred rite,
In elusive solitude's sweet light.

The world goes on, yet here I stay,
In quiet realms where few will stray.
I grasp the moment, never fleeting,
In stillness found, my soul completing.

Nature's Glacial Muse

Beneath the frost, the silence sings,
Whispers of peace on crystal wings.
In every flake, a story weaves,
Nature's brush, as winter leaves.

Mountains etched in icy grace,
Soft reflections, a frozen trace.
In quiet woods, the breath of stars,
Nature's muse, with all its scars.

The streams run cold, yet full of life,
A balance sought amidst the strife.
Each branch adorned, a glistening charm,
In nature's hold, I find my calm.

Underneath the pale blue sky,
The hoot of owls, a lullaby.
The crystal world, so bright, so vast,
A fleeting breath of winter's past.

In every corner, beauty lies,
Captured shades of dawn arise.
With every step, a story unfolds,
Nature's glacial muse, untold.

Serene Icy Visions

In the hush of morning's light,
The world transformed, so pure, so bright.
Beneath the veil of soft white snow,
Serene visions begin to flow.

Crystal branches, twinkling bright,
Nature swathed in gentle light.
The air is crisp, the heart is still,
In icy realms, I find my will.

A tranquil lake, a mirror clear,
Reflecting dreams that draw me near.
With every breath, a tranquil sigh,
In these serene moments, I fly.

The silence sings of winter's grace,
In soft embrace, I find my place.
With every flake, a vision cast,
In stillness found, I breathe at last.

Ethereal shades dance in the frost,
In fleeting moments, never lost.
In icy visions, beauty reigns,
A peaceful heart, in gentle chains.

Ethereal Chill

In twilight's glow, a whisper calls,
Ethereal chill through shadowed halls.
With every sigh, the starlight glows,
A dance of frost where silence flows.

The moon hangs low, a guiding light,
Illuminating the tranquil night.
Each breath a cloud, a fleeting sail,
In chilly moments, I prevail.

The world in slumber, wrapped in white,
A peaceful pause, a sweet delight.
With every heartbeat, time stands still,
In ethereal chill, I find my thrill.

The winds carry tales of yore,
In frosted whispers, wisdom's core.
The icy breath of winter's hand,
An ethereal touch across the land.

With layers thick and skies so clear,
The beauty blooms, it draws me near.
In frozen breaths, my spirit flies,
In ethereal chill beneath the skies.

A Prism of Solitude

In corners deep, where shadows play,
A quiet heart finds room to sway.
Each whispered thought, all softly spun,
Reflects the light of a setting sun.

Alone, but not in empty plight,
The stillness holds a gleaming sight.
With every breath, the silence sings,
A world revealed in hidden wings.

The echoes dance on walls of gray,
In solitude, the mind will stray.
A prism's glow takes form anew,
In fractured light, a bursting hue.

Rays bend and twist through cracks of time,
In quiet moments, thoughts will climb.
Each fractured beam, a tale to share,
Embracing peace in evening air.

The night unveils a softer glow,
Where secrets linger, dreams will flow.
In solitude, the soul finds peace,
An artful calm, a sweet release.

Frosted Dreams Unraveled

Beneath the glint of winter's breath,
A dream wrapped tight in icy wreath.
Each crystal shard a story told,
In frosty whispers, bright and bold.

The world, a canvas, sleek and white,
Where visions dance in borrowed light.
With every flake, a wish sent high,
In frozen realms, where echoes lie.

Laughter sparkles in the air,
As dreams unfold with tender care.
In chilling winds, our hopes arise,
A frosted tale beneath the skies.

With each dawn, the shimmer fades,
Yet warmth remains in frozen glades.
Unraveled dreams in sunlight stream,
Casting hope on winter's beam.

The frost may bite, the world may chill,
Yet within dreams, we find our will.
In shimmering nights, our hearts will soar,
To chase the light forevermore.

Silent Enchantment

In twilight hours, where silence weaves,
The air is thick with magic leaves.
A gentle hush enchants the night,
While stars above ignite the sight.

Each breath of wind tells tales untold,
Of lives entwined in dreams of old.
In whispered tones, the shadows blend,
A spell is cast, where moments mend.

The moonlight drapes a silver cloak,
As nature breathes, and spirits soak.
In quiet woods, the heart will race,
Embracing peace in hidden space.

With each flicker of a distant light,
The world transforms, as day to night.
In tranquil walks, we lose our fears,
As silent magic draws us near.

The stars will wink, a knowing glance,
Inviting us to join the dance.
In silent enchantment, souls take flight,
In whispers soft, we taste the night.

Chilled Murmurs

In crisp dawn's breath, the world awakes,
Chilled murmurs stir as silence breaks.
Each rustle brings the frost's soft kiss,
In tender hues, a morning bliss.

Whispers drift on icy air,
As nature hums, a secret fair.
With every step, the crunching sound,
Paints winter's song upon the ground.

The branches sway with frosted grace,
In quiet, still, a peaceful space.
The murmurs weave between the trees,
An ancient song upon the breeze.

With soft serenity in sight,
Each chilled breath ignites the night.
In echoes deep, the heart will yearn,
For whispered truths, for tides to turn.

As twilight comes, the murmur dims,
Yet in the dark, the secret swims.
Through chilled airs, we find our way,
In softest dreams, we choose to stay.

Winter's Silken Caress

Snowflakes dance on whispered air,
Each a secret, light and rare.
Blankets soft upon the ground,
A hush of peace, so lightly found.

Frosted branches, silvered sheen,
Nature's jewels, bright and keen.
A world transformed, serene and bright,
In the arms of winter's night.

Breath of chill, yet warmth inside,
Hearts entwined, no need to hide.
With every step, a crunch of snow,
In winter's hush, our spirits grow.

Icicles hang, crystal clear,
Laughter echoes, joy and cheer.
The fire crackles, stories shared,
In this embrace, we're unprepared.

As dawn approaches, colors bloom,
Golden rays dispel the gloom.
Winter fades, yet memories stay,
In winter's silken, sweet ballet.

Translucent Reveries

In the morn, the mist will rise,
Softly cloaking earth's surprise.
Whispers of the dreams we keep,
In translucent shades, we leap.

Gentle winds through branches weave,
Carrying tales that we believe.
Each horizon holds a spark,
Noting paths where shadows hark.

Floating gently, thoughts entwined,
In every moment, peace we find.
Reflections dance upon the lake,
Translucent dreams, awake, awake!

Beneath the sky, we hold our breath,
Life's a canvas, love the brush.
Colors of longing touch the heart,
In these reveries, we won't part.

As evening falls, the stars ignite,
Translucent dreams in the night.
A tapestry of wishes made,
In the quiet, we won't fade.

Fragments of Ice

Shattered glimmers catch the sun,
Life's reflections, on the run.
Tiny crystals, pure and bright,
Whisper stories lost to night.

Each fragment tells of winter's breath,
A fleeting dance, the chill of death.
Yet in their glint, a memory,
Of warmth and love, a tapestry.

Frozen rivers, silent flow,
Every movement, soft and slow.
Carved by time, a fleeting grace,
Fragments of ice, nature's embrace.

Underneath, the world lies still,
Waiting for the thaw, the thrill.
Winter's grasp begins to wane,
In broken pieces, life remains.

As seasons turn, the ice will break,
Revealing paths that we will take.
Through fragments, we shall see the light,
In every shard, a future bright.

The Quiet Tapestry

Threads of silence linger near,
Woven whispers, soft and clear.
Each stitch holds a tale untold,
In colors rich, and textures bold.

The loom of life spins day by day,
Weaving dreams in hues of gray.
In quiet moments, beauty grows,
In every pause, love overflows.

Patterns shift, as seasons change,
Embroidered hopes, both wide and strange.
Each loop a bond, each knot a tear,
In the tapestry, we lay bare.

Gentle hands with tender care,
Crafting comforts, always there.
Through trials faced, we mend, restore,
In the quiet, hearts explore.

As twilight falls, the colors blend,
Life's tapestry will never end.
In silence, we find strength anew,
A canvas rich in every hue.

Twinkling Icicles

Hanging from the eaves, so bright,
Glistening in the pale moonlight.
Silent drips from frozen streams,
Nature's art in winter dreams.

Each shard reflects the starry night,
A symphony of cold, pure light.
They dance upon the breath of air,
Whispering secrets, soft and rare.

Beneath the weight of winter's grace,
Icicles shimmer in their place.
A fragile world, so still, so clear,
Holding time's breath, holding near.

With every dawn, they start to sway,
As sunlight kisses cold away.
Yet in their glimmer, hope does stay,
For spring will find its gentle way.

So marvel at their beauty here,
These twinkling gems we hold so dear.
A fleeting moment, then they're gone,
But memories linger, brightly shone.

Chillin' Clarity

The air is crisp, the world is clear,
Whispers of winter draw us near.
Frost lies thick on every tree,
Nature's breath, so pure, so free.

Sound of crunching underfoot,
Blankets of snow, the world is mute.
Clouds of white against the blue,
A tranquil scene, so bright and true.

Frozen lakes like mirrors gleam,
Reflecting life, a tranquil dream.
The chill invites a warming heart,
In every corner, winter's art.

Clear as glass, the world anew,
Colors pop in vibrant hue.
Bundle up, let laughter soar,
In chilling clarity, explore.

A world reborn in diamond light,
Wrap yourself in warmth tonight.
As stars emerge and twilight glows,
Cherish winter, as it grows.

Poetry Beneath the Snow

Silent verses, soft and low,
Whispers held beneath the snow.
Each flake a word, each drift a rhyme,
Nature's poem, inching time.

Blanket wide, a velvet spread,
Stitching peace where footsteps tread.
In this hush, a tale unfolds,
Of frozen dreams and stories told.

Muffled laughter in the air,
Children's joy, they dance without care.
Imprints left in glistening white,
Echoes of day until the night.

Branches bow under the weight,
Crystals form at winter's gate.
Each moment penned in icy prose,
Life, it freezes, yet still flows.

For beneath the cold, a fire will grow,
In every heart where love can glow.
In winter's arms, we find our way,
As poetry lives, even in gray.

Harmonies of Winter

In whispers soft, the winter sings,
Chilled melodies on frosty wings.
Crisp notes dance in the bracing air,
Harmonies rise without a care.

The trees sway gently, bowing low,
As if in awe of winter's show.
Stars above twinkle like a choir,
Each sparkle fuels the heart's desire.

The wind, a flute, plays through the night,
A serenade in silver light.
Snowflakes twirl like dancers free,
Painting joy in pure esprit.

With every breath, a note appears,
A symphony that calms our fears.
Feel the chill, embrace the calm,
Nature's song is life's sweet balm.

As days grow short and evenings long,
Let winter's beauty hum its song.
For in the cold, there's warmth to find,
In harmonies of winter, intertwined.

The Beauty of an Icy Embrace

In silence wraps the winter night,
A chill that whispers, soft and light.
Embrace the frost, a gentle kiss,
In icy realms, we find our bliss.

With every breath, a crystal form,
Painting landscapes, pure and warm.
Underneath the pale moon's glow,
Nature's art begins to show.

The trees stand tall, a silver hue,
Adorned in diamonds, bright and true.
Each branch a promise, bending low,
In frosty arms, the quiet grows.

As time stands still, the world gives pause,
A beauty swathed in winter's cause.
Each flake that falls, a soft embrace,
In icy wonder, we find grace.

Poetry Found in Crystal Tides

The waves of winter gently kiss,
A shore adorned in frosty bliss.
With every tide, the sea does weave,
A tapestry of dreams we breathe.

Each crystal flake like whispered word,
A quiet echo, softly heard.
In frozen dance, the waters gleam,
Expressing all, a silent dream.

From shores of ice, the songs arise,
Mirroring the starlit skies.
The ocean speaks in tones so bright,
In shivering form, it takes flight.

In every breath, the sea's embrace,
A rhythm found in crystal grace.
Let poetry flow, let verses glide,
In winter's heart, there's joy inside.

Enchanted Frost Beneath the Stars

Beneath the stars, a world revealed,
In frosted whispers, dreams concealed.
The night, a cloak of silver light,
Enchantment stirs in snowy flight.

The trees wear coats of glimmering white,
Each branch a stroke of nature's might.
A dance of shadows, soft and free,
In these dark depths, we long to see.

While starlight twinkles, pure and bright,
It paints the earth in cosmic light.
The frost, a magic, serene and mild,
Invokes the wonder of the wild.

As night deepens, the world feels close,
In icy charm, our hearts propose.
To wander lost in dreams above,
In winter's hold, we find our love.

Glistening Hues of a Winter's Dream

In hues of blue and silver streams,
The winter paints the land with dreams.
Golden light on crystal ground,
In every spark, a magic found.

The morning sun, a gentle rise,
Reflects in diamonds, bright surprise.
With every glance, a story spun,
Of winter's chill and warming sun.

Among the whispers of the trees,
In every gust, a secret breeze.
The tranquil air, a soothing balm,
In frosty stillness, we find calm.

Each moment crafted, pure delight,
In nature's arms, the soul takes flight.
To wander through these glistening seams,
Is to embrace winter's dreaming themes.

Fractured Light on a Quiet Lake

Moonlight dances on the waves,
Whispers of the night surround.
Ripples catch the silver glow,
In the stillness, peace is found.

Stars above in quiet grace,
Reflect on waters deep and clear.
Nature's canvas, painted bright,
Holds the secrets of the year.

Gentle breezes softly sweep,
Rustling leaves in twilight's hold.
Fractured beams of luminous dreams,
Secrets of the lake unfold.

Time stands still beneath the sky,
Every moment, pure delight.
In this realm where echoes fade,
Fractured light sets souls alight.

Here, an echo of the day,
Merging with the night's embrace.
On this quiet, tranquil lake,
Life finds rhythm, finds its place.

Echoes of a Snowbound Heart

Blankets white on slumbering ground,
Silent whispers fill the air.
Footprints lost, the past is found,
In the hush, a frozen stare.

Crimson berries 'gainst the white,
Life's bold colors stand apart.
Winter's chill, yet warm inside,
Echoes of a snowbound heart.

Branches bare, adorned with frost,
A canvas made of dreams and sighs.
In this world, we count the cost,
Where the coldest memory lies.

Fires burn bright with tales retold,
Of love lost in the swirling snow.
Winter holds what cannot fold,
Echoes soft, forever flow.

Yet in this white, a spark ignites,
Hope awakens, takes its flight.
Echoes of a heart once bold,
Find their warmth in winter's night.

Shimmering Shadows Beneath the Frost

Underneath the icy veil,
Shadows dance and secrets hide.
In the stillness of the night,
Life whispers where dreams abide.

Crystals form on branches bare,
Nature's art in pale moonlight.
Every shimmer, sheer delight,
Beneath the frost, a world of light.

Footsteps soft on crunchy ground,
Echoes move as whispers play.
In this tranquil battleground,
Shimmering shadows softly sway.

Every breath, a cloud of mist,
Painting tales on winter air.
In the quiet, love persists,
Amidst the shadows, hearts laid bare.

When day breaks, the frost will yield,
Yet memories will survive.
In the shimmering, shadows sealed,
Winter's magic will contrive.

The Soul of a Winter's Night

Stars arrayed like diamonds bright,
In the vast and endless dome.
Winter whispers through the night,
Calling wanderers to roam.

Frosty breath in cool night air,
Carries tales of worlds unknown.
Listen close, if you dare,
Find the warmth in each cold stone.

Silhouettes of trees stand tall,
Guardians of secrets and dreams.
In their shadows, shadows fall,
Wrapped in whispered, silent themes.

The moon's soft glow illuminates,
Paths where hearts brave the stillness.
Finding peace, the soul creates,
Moments drenched in quiet thrillness.

Beneath this cold, the warmth ignites,
Finding love within the night.
In winter's grip, we're all entwined,
The soul of night, forever kind.

Frigid Lullabies

In the still of night, the cold winds weep,
Underneath the stars, they softly creep.
Snowflakes dance like dreams untold,
Whispers of secrets, ancient and bold.

A blanket of silence, a world so white,
Cradled in slumber, the moon takes flight.
Each breath a cloud, each heartbeat a song,
In frigid lullabies, we all belong.

Trees wear their coats of shimmering ice,
Nature sings softly, a wonder device.
Glistening echoes in the frostbitten air,
Melodies linger, enchanting and rare.

The night holds its secrets, wrapped up in dreams,
A tapestry woven with silvered seams.
Frigid lullabies in the depths of the night,
Guide us to calm, where shadows take flight.

Shards of Stillness

In the quiet corners where shadows play,
Fragments of silence drift softly away.
Time stands still on this crystal clear,
Each shard of stillness whispers near.

Beneath the surface, the echoes reside,
Captured in moments, where secrets abide.
A frozen lake with stories untold,
Shards of stillness, with memories old.

The air is thick with the weight of the night,
Glimmers of starlight, a shimmering sight.
Echoes of laughter, now lost in the cold,
Shards of stillness, like treasures of gold.

Each breath is a pause, each heartbeat a chance,
In the dance of atoms, a slow, gentle trance.
Nature's embrace in a beautiful reel,
Shards of stillness, forever they steal.

The Enchanted Reflector

In twilight's embrace, reflections appear,
Mirrors of magic, so vividly clear.
Where shadows mingle and secrets are shared,
The enchanted reflector, forever ensnared.

Beneath the surface, the stories unfold,
With colors and dreams, both vibrant and bold.
In pools of the past, we glimpse our own fate,
The enchanted reflector will never wait.

A dance of the light, a flicker of souls,
Illuminating paths, as the nighttime unfolds.
Each gaze is a journey to realms yet unseen,
The enchanted reflector, a bridge to the dream.

Time waltzes on, with a soft, subtle tease,
In the mirror's embrace, the heart finds its ease.
Glimmers of truth in the moon's gentle glow,
The enchanted reflector, forever we'll know.

Whispering Frost

In the hush of dawn, where silence breathes,
Whispering frost weaves delicate wreaths.
Each crystal a tale, a moment in time,
Nature's soft chorus, a lyrical chime.

Beneath the pale moon, the world holds its breath,
In frosty embraces, we dance with death.
Fragile yet bold, the beauty it brings,
Whispering frost sings of forgotten things.

The trees stand tall, adorned with their lace,
Embroidered with dreams, they're touched by grace.
Glimmers of silver in a world so vast,
Whispering frost, a spell that holds fast.

Echoes of winters long past fill the air,
Wrapped up in magic, all hearts will share.
In the still of the morn, the beauty is lost,
To the lull of the whispers, we pay the cost.

Mirage of Snowflakes in Twilight

Soft whispers dance through the air,
As twilight settles with graceful flair.
Snowflakes twirl like fleeting dreams,
In a world where nothing's as it seems.

Pale beams of dusk paint the skies,
While winter's breath endlessly sighs.
Each flake a story softly spun,
In the warmth of day, now comes undone.

The ground adorned with a silken sheet,
Footprints vanish where shadows meet.
Glimmers of silver, a fleeting show,
A temporary beauty in soft, cold glow.

Hushed are the whispers of the night,
As echoes carry the fading light.
Twists and turns in the dimming land,
Hold the secrets of time in hand.

In the twilight's embrace, we drift away,
Chasing dreams until break of day.
Miraged moments in frosty air,
Eternal echoes, fleeting and rare.

Reflections of Light Through Darkened Ice

Cold fingers trace on glassy sheet,
Captured moments, bittersweet.
Light fractures through in rainbowed hues,
A dance of colors, the heart ensues.

Beneath the surface, shadows dwell,
Whispers held in an icy shell.
Fragments of sorrow, lost and free,
Reflected stories, you and me.

Silent echoes float like dreams,
Trapped in frost, or so it seems.
Each glimmer holds a hidden tale,
Of distant echoes, of love, of frail.

Crystals shimmer in fleeting time,
Lingering soft in the quiet climb.
Gentle layers of the forgotten past,
In the stillness waiting, yet so vast.

Time stands still in this frozen grace,
Where light and darkness softly embrace.
Reflections whisper as night draws near,
In the silence, we listen, we hear.

Traces of Warmth in Winter's Grasp

Beneath the veil of the frosty night,
Small embers glow with tender light.
Whispers of warmth seep through the cold,
In the heart's chamber, stories unfold.

Each breath a cloud, soft and white,
As warmth battles the bitter bite.
Hidden refuges, hearts entwined,
In winter's hold, our love defined.

Footsteps crunch on the snow-clad ground,
Echoes of laughter in silence found.
Moments of joy wrapped in the chill,
As two souls wander, time stands still.

Sunrise breaks with a golden hue,
Painting the world in colors anew.
In winter's grasp, hope holds its place,
As warmth holds steady, a sweet embrace.

With every season, love's light will stay,
Through the frost, come what may.
Traces of warmth in a world so vast,
Illuminate paths, where shadows are cast.

Shivering Echoes of Time

Through corridors of frost and chill,
Life moves slowly, yet in thrill.
Whispers linger in the icy air,
Shivering echoes of moments rare.

Each tick of time paints shadows deep,
As hearts awaken from frozen sleep.
Silent stories blend and entwine,
In the tapestry of the divine.

Frost on the window, patterns intricate,
Each design a memory delicate.
In the stillness, we find our pace,
Tracing the paths of winter's embrace.

Echoes of laughter, lost in the past,
In the softness of dusk, they forever last.
Silent witnesses to dreams once bright,
Now scattered through the shivering night.

Yet with each dawn, a promise made,
To cherish the light where shadows fade.
In the heart's echo, time finds its way,
Guiding us gently to another day.